Foreword

Melanie hated being the center of attention. In fact, she went to great lengths to avoid it. Because of that, we didn't know the extent of her involvement in the community. Person after person came up to us and talked about the role she played in organizations that we didn't know she had any interest in, let alone had leadership positions. She had a vibrant life full of friends and volunteerism that we didn't know about. She was a blessing in more lives than we ever imagined.

I have never known anyone quite like her, and as impressed as I was, it doesn't hold a candle to the woman I learned she was. And I am certain I still only know a small part of what she accomplished, what was important to her, and all that should be remembered of her.

For that reason, this book was almost titled "What I Want To Know About You". But thinking of my sister made me realize there are many parts of a person's life they want to keep to themselves or just for certain people. So instead, it changed to reflect that this desire to be known comes directly from the one answering the questions. Whether they picked the book up themselves or received it as a gift, they are giving this knowledge back to their loved ones and learning about themselves in the process.

Foreword

This is the book, well actually the companion book, that I have been trying to put together for years and finally over the last couple of months had set a deadline to finish in 2023 — but I just couldn't get the motivation to start. Because I write to feel a personal connection, and I had yet to really understand how important something like this could be for a loved one.

Then the unthinkable happened: my sister, Melanie, passed away on January 2, 2023. It was completely unexpected, it was completely heartbreaking, and it was completely eye opening.

We had what I consider a normal big-sister little-brother relationship. There were things I knew that no one else did, but we were not as close as I wished in hindsight. In the weeks that followed as we prepared for her memorial, I learned that there were huge gaps in my knowledge, in the knowledge of her son, her parents (who both survived her), and that of my wife and daughters (all of whom were also very close to her). We all had a window into who she was, but it was like each window was looking into a different room. And we all found out there were rooms that we had no idea even existed until after her passing. I think each of us in our own ways underestimated the vibrancy of her life. We were only looking through our own little windows, so we had no idea that her life was not a tiny house but rather a mansion of complexity and connectivity.

Foreword

While for many this book may be left as a gift after your death,
I hope some of these stories will be shared in your lifetime.
Bringing to life these real moments can bring you closer to your
loved ones. But I also know that many of the answers in this book
will be read posthumously, where they may add color to your life
and give direction to readers.

Just know that I hope you enjoy the process of filling these pages
and that your readers will cherish your words.

HOW TO USE THE BOOK

First, this is written for a broad audience, so some questions and even some sections may not apply. If that is the case for you, just skip them.

This will be written as if one person is answering each question, but I also suspect that often a couple may be answering together. I will try to leave enough space for two people to answer, just make sure it's clear whose answer is whose. For example, birthdays may be easier, but personal responses should keep a consistent format that is easy to follow. You could use two ink colors or mark the start of each person's answer with their initials. No matter what you decide, make sure you stay consistent throughout the book.

You will start with the easy biographical information and work your way into things that may give insight into who you are and what you like, ending with your hopes for the person(s) who will read this book.

HOW TO USE THE BOOK

Finally, as mentioned above, there may be parts of the book that don't apply, but there may also be parts you don't want to answer here. Skip them for now and you can always revisit them later. It's ok if you don't want to answer something; anything that you do share will be appreciated by whoever reads this book.

Let's get started!

Name(s)

_____

Who Is This For

_____

Date Started

_____

Date Completed

_____

Table of Contents

Chapter 1 - Just the Facts

OK, this the driest chapter. No stories, no cute anecdotes. As this chapter title reads, it is just the facts. Necessary but probably not the most exciting section of the book. So for you the writer, just do it. For you the reader, there are probably some nuggets you will want to know, but reading it word for word may be a bit much. So peruse it and move on, and then if you have questions, jump back to it.

Your Legal Name

Your Given Nickname

(Do I like it, hate it, and is there a story attached?)

Your Chosen Nickname

(Is there a story attached?)

Birthdate

Your Age As Of Today

_____

_____

Weight

Height

_____

_____

Hair Color

_____

Where were you born?

_____

Where did you grow up?
(If different)

_____

Who was your best friend growing up?

_____

Are you still in touch?

_____

Who is your best friend currently?

_____

Phone Number   Email Address

_____   _____

Where do you live now?

_____

Describe yourself to someone you are meeting for the first time
so that they could recognize you.

_____

_____

_____

_____

_____

_____

Distinguishing Features:

_____

_____

_____

_____

_____

_____

_____

_____

_____

Do you (or did you) have an accent? If so, where from?

_____

Your Parents

Names   Where Were They Born?

_____   _____

_____   _____

Are They Still Living? If Passed, When?

_____

_____

Any Other Parental Information

_____

_____

Your Grandparents

Names   Where Were They Born?

_____   _____

_____   _____

Are They Still Living? If Passed, When?

_____

_____

Any Other Family Elders Information

_____

_____

Your Siblings

Names   Where Were They Born?

_____   _____

_____   _____

_____   _____

Are They Still Living? If Passed, When?

_____

Any Other Family Information

_____

_____

Your Marital Status

_____

Your Significant Other(s)

Names   Where Were They Born?

_____   _____

Are They Still Living? If Passed, When?

_____

Any Other Significant Others Information

_____

_____

Religion

_____

Is this the same as your parents/grandparents?
If not, what was theirs?

_____

_____

_____

Has your religion changed during your life time? If so, why?

_____

_____

_____

_____

_____

_____

_____

_____

_____

_____

_____

_____

_____

_____

_____

Race

_____

Ethnicity

_____

Political Affiliation

_____

Is your political affiliation the same as your parents/grandparents?
If not what was theirs?

_____

_____

Has your political affiliation changed during your lifetime?
If so, why?

_____

_____

_____

_____

_____

_____

_____

_____

_____

_____

Information that you want to highlight, ran out of space answering, or additional information that was not asked or needed more space.

_____

_____

_____

_____

_____

_____

_____

_____

_____

_____

_____

_____

_____

_____

_____

_____

_____

_____

_____

_____

_____

_____

_____

Chapter 2 - Relationships

The Ones You Chose And The Ones You Didn't.
Let's Start With The Personal.

What was the most important relationship in your life?

_____

Is there a relationship that you regret?
Why and what would you have done differently?

_____
_____
_____
_____
_____
_____
_____
_____
_____
_____
_____
_____
_____
_____
_____
_____
_____
_____
_____

Tell me about your first romantic relationship.
When was it, and what was it like?

_____
_____
_____
_____
_____
_____
_____
_____
_____

Was there a love of your life? If so, who and how did the relationship proceed?

_____
_____
_____
_____
_____
_____
_____
_____
_____
_____
_____
_____
_____
_____
_____

What qualities did you look for in a partner when you were younger and did those qualities change as you got older?

_____
_____
_____
_____
_____

How did you meet your spouse?

_____
_____
_____
_____

What were some of the biggest challenges you faced in your romantic relationships?

_____
_____
_____
_____
_____
_____
_____
_____
_____
_____
_____
_____

How were you able to overcome those challenges?

_____

_____

_____

_____

_____

_____

What were some of the biggest challenges you faced in your social relationships?

_____

_____

_____

_____

_____

Were you able to overcome the challenges and if so, how?

_____

_____

_____

_____

_____

_____

_____

_____

_____

How did you work through conflicts or disagreements with your partner? Did it change over time?

_____

_____

_____

_____

_____

_____

_____

_____

What were some of the most important values in your relationships?

_____

_____

_____

_____

_____

_____

_____

_____

_____

_____

_____

_____

_____

What role did communication play in your relationships?

_____

_____

_____

_____

_____

_____

_____

How did your relationships changed over time?

_____

_____

_____

_____

_____

_____

_____

_____

_____

_____

_____

_____

_____

Did you have any significant breakups? What did you learned from them?

_____

_____

_____

_____

_____

_____

_____

_____

_____

_____

How did you navigate changes in your relationships
(such as moving or starting a family)?

_____

_____

_____

_____

_____

_____

_____

_____

_____

_____

_____

What was the most difficult decision you had to make in a relationship?

_____

_____

_____

_____

_____

_____

_____

_____

_____

_____

_____

_____

How has your family influenced your relationships?

_____

_____

_____

_____

_____

_____

_____

_____

_____

_____

_____

Did you have any cultural norms you had to (or chose to) adhere to in your relationship? If so, what were they?

_____

_____

_____

_____

_____

_____

_____

_____

_____

_____

What role did friendships play in your romantic relationship?

_____

_____

_____

_____

_____

_____

_____

_____

_____

_____

_____

_____

_____

_____

Did you ever experience heartbreak or loss in a relationship?
Did that affect future relationships and how?

_____

_____

_____

_____

_____

_____

_____

_____

What advice would you give to someone starting a new relationship?

_____

_____

_____

How did your children or grandchildren affect your romantic relationships?

_____

_____

_____

_____

_____

_____

_____

What was the most important thing you learned about relationships over time?

_____

_____

_____

_____

_____

_____

_____

_____

_____

How did your relationships impact your career or other aspects of your life?
Did you ever have to choose between them, and if so, which one did
you choose, and do you regret it?

_____

_____

_____

_____

_____

_____

_____

_____

_____

_____

What role did trust play in your relationships?

_____

_____

_____

_____

_____

_____

_____

_____

_____

_____

_____

_____

_____

_____

How did you balance your personal goals and interests
with those of your partner?

_____

_____

_____

_____

_____

_____

_____

_____

_____

_____

Did you ever have to deal with jealousy or broken trust in a relationship? How did you handle it?

What was the most important lesson you learned about
yourself through your relationships?

_____

_____

_____

_____

_____

_____

_____

_____

_____

_____

_____

How did your relationships shape the person you are today?

_____

_____

_____

_____

_____

_____

_____

_____

_____

Looking back, what wasn't important in your relationships
that you thought was important at the time?

_____

_____

_____

_____

_____

_____

What was important that you wished you realized earlier?

_____

_____

_____

_____

_____

_____

_____

_____

_____

What would you have done differently in your relationships?

_____

_____

_____

_____

_____

_____

Now on to families:

Describe your relationship with your mother:

_____

_____

_____

_____

_____

_____

_____

_____

_____

Was there something you wish would have been different,
or **could** have done differently?

_____

_____

_____

_____

_____

_____

_____

Describe your relationship with your father:

_____

_____

_____

_____

_____

_____

_____

_____

_____

_____

_____

Was there something you wish would have been different,
or that you could have done differently?

_____

_____

_____

_____

_____

_____

_____

_____

_____

_____

_____

Describe your relationship with your siblings (as a group or individually):

_____

_____

_____

_____

_____

_____

_____

_____

_____

Was there something you wish would have been different,
or could have done differently?

_____

_____

_____

_____

_____

_____

_____

_____

_____

Describe any other significant family relationship.
Why was this person chosen?

_____

_____

_____

_____

_____

_____

_____

_____

_____

_____

_____

_____

_____

_____

_____

_____

_____

_____

_____

_____

_____

Now on to Friends:

Who are your best friends?

_____

_____

Why are they your best friends?

_____

_____

_____

_____

_____

_____

_____

_____

_____

_____

_____

_____

_____

_____

Why do you define them as your best friends?

_____

_____

_____

_____

_____

_____

How long have you been friends?

_____

What do you value most about them?

_____

_____

_____

_____

_____

_____

_____

What do you value most about the relationship?

_____

_____

_____

_____

Is there a key trait that you look for in a friend?

_____

_____

_____

_____

_____

Was there someone who you would have named previously as a best friend that you wouldn't now? If so, who is it and why are you no longer best friends?

_____

_____

_____

_____

_____

_____

_____

Who has had the most significant impact on you and why (not career related)?

_____

_____

_____

_____

_____

_____

Information that you want to highlight, ran out of space answering, or additional information that was not asked or needed more space.

_____

_____

_____

_____

_____

_____

_____

_____

_____

_____

_____

_____

_____

_____

_____

_____

_____

_____

_____

_____

_____

_____

_____

_____

_____

Chapter 3 - Beyond The Facts: What Made You?

(Or at least your version of it.)

Tell me about your career.

_____

_____

_____

_____

_____

_____

_____

_____

_____

What inspired you to pursue the career path that you did, or
did you just fall into it, and how?

_____

_____

_____

_____

_____

_____

_____

Do you wish you followed a different career path, and if so, why didn't you?

_____

_____

_____

_____

_____

_____

Describe the most rewarding experience in your career.

_____

_____

_____

_____

_____

_____

_____

_____

_____

_____

_____

_____

_____

_____

_____

_____

_____

_____

Name at least 2 of the biggest challenges you faced in your career.
How did you overcome them?

1. _____

_____

_____

_____

_____

_____

_____

_____

_____

_____

_____

2. _____

_____

_____

_____

_____

_____

_____

_____

_____

_____

_____

_____

_____

What motivates or motivated you to keep working throughout your career?

_____

_____

_____

_____

_____

_____

_____

_____

_____

_____

_____

How did you balance work and personal life when you
were working, and did you find the right balance?

_____

_____

_____

_____

_____

_____

_____

_____

_____

_____

_____

_____

What advice would you give to someone just starting out in any industry
What advice would you give to someone just starting out in your specific industry?

_____
_____
_____
_____
_____
_____
_____
_____
_____

What skills do you think are most important to succeed at work?

_____
_____
_____
_____
_____
_____
_____
_____
_____
_____
_____
_____
_____
_____

Did you have multiple careers? If yes, why?

_____

_____

_____

_____

_____

_____

_____

_____

_____

_____

_____

_____

How did your industry change during your career?

_____

_____

_____

_____

_____

_____

_____

_____

_____

_____

_____

_____

_____

_____

Did you have any mentors or role models that helped you along the way?

_____

_____

_____

_____

_____

_____

_____

_____

What was the most important lesson you learned during your career?

_____

_____

_____

_____

_____

_____

_____

_____

_____

_____

_____

_____

_____

_____

What was the biggest mistake you made in your
career, and what did you learn from it?

What was the most significant project you worked on in your career?
Did you realize it at the time?

_____

_____

_____

_____

_____

_____

_____

_____

_____

_____

_____

Describe a time when you had to make a difficult decision in your career.
Why it was difficult?

_____

_____

_____

_____

_____

_____

_____

_____

_____

What was your biggest accomplishment during your career?

_____
_____
_____
_____
_____
_____
_____
_____
_____
_____
_____
_____
_____

What was your favorite part of your job?

_____
_____
_____
_____
_____
_____
_____
_____
_____
_____
_____
_____
_____
_____

How did you stay up-to-date with industry trends
and changes throughout your career?

_____
_____
_____
_____
_____
_____
_____
_____
_____
_____
_____

What was the most valuable piece of advice you ever
received about your career?

_____
_____
_____
_____
_____
_____
_____
_____
_____
_____

Describe a time when you had to take a risk in your career.
How did it turn out?

Describe **another** time when you had to take a risk in your
career. How did it turn out?

_____

_____

_____

_____

_____

_____

_____

_____

_____

_____

_____

_____

What were some of the key skills you needed to have a successful career?

_____

_____

_____

_____

_____

_____

_____

_____

_____

_____

_____

How did you handle difficult colleagues or bosses during your career?

_____

_____

_____

_____

_____

_____

_____

_____

_____

_____

_____

_____

How did you balance work and family responsibilities?

_____

_____

_____

_____

_____

_____

_____

_____

_____

Did you ever consider changing careers?

_____

_____

_____

_____

_____

_____

_____

_____

What would you have done differently in your career if you had the chance?

_____

_____

_____

_____

_____

_____

_____

_____

_____

_____

_____

_____

_____

_____

_____

_____

_____

_____

What legacy do you hope to leave from your career?

Did you have a mentor? If so, how did they come to be your mentor?

_____

_____

_____

_____

_____

_____

_____

_____

_____

_____

_____

What was the most important feature of that relationship?

_____

_____

_____

_____

_____

_____

_____

_____

_____

_____

Tell me about your family

Tell me about your parents:

_____
_____
_____
_____
_____
_____
_____
_____
_____
_____
_____
_____
_____
_____
_____
_____
_____
_____
_____
_____
_____
_____
_____
_____
_____
_____
_____
_____

What is the one thing you wish everyone knew about your mother?

_____
_____
_____
_____
_____
_____
_____
_____
_____
_____
_____
_____
_____

What is the one thing you wished everyone knew about your father?

_____
_____
_____
_____
_____
_____
_____
_____
_____
_____
_____
_____
_____
_____

Do you have any siblings?

_____

What is the one thing you wish everyone knew about each of your siblings?

_____
_____
_____
_____
_____
_____
_____
_____
_____
_____
_____
_____
_____
_____
_____

What is your birth order among your siblings?

_____
_____
_____

What is your relationship with your siblings like today?

_____

_____

_____

_____

_____

_____

_____

_____

_____

_____

_____

Do you have any step-siblings or half-siblings?

_____

_____

_____

Are your parents still together or divorced?

_____

_____

What was your upbringing like?
Could you tell a story that you feel describes your upbringing?
If you can't think of a story, what TV/movie family do you
think most closely resembles yours?

Did you grow up in a large or small family?

_____

_____

_____

_____

_____

_____

_____

_____

_____

_____

_____

_____

Do you have any extended family members that you are close to?

_____

_____

_____

_____

_____

_____

_____

_____

_____

Do you have any family traditions? What are they?
Do you still carry them on and/or do other family members?

_____

_____

_____

_____

_____

_____

_____

_____

_____

_____

_____

_____

Is there a family tradition you didn't like growing up, but that you now carry on?

_____

_____

_____

_____

_____

_____

_____

Is there a new family tradition that you started? What is it and why?

_____

_____

_____

_____

_____

_____

_____

_____

_____

_____

_____

_____

What was your favorite family vacation or trip growing up? Did your family
have a special place they visited? Or a special type of trip they took?

_____

_____

_____

_____

_____

_____

_____

_____

_____

_____

_____

_____

Do you have any family members who have passed away that were particularly important to you? And if so, why?

Have there been any significant events in your
family's history that have impacted you ?

_____

_____

_____

_____

_____

_____

_____

_____

_____

How has your family shaped who you are as a person?

_____

_____

_____

_____

_____

_____

_____

_____

_____

_____

_____

Do you have any unique or interesting family stories?

Have you ever found out your family history, whether from your
own research or learning from other family members?
If you did, what did you learn?

Do you have any family heirlooms that are important to you? Why?

_____

_____

_____

_____

_____

_____

_____

_____

_____

_____

Do you have any family members who have served in the military?

_____

_____

_____

_____

Are there any family recipes that have been passed down through generations? What are they?

_____

_____

_____

_____

_____

Has your family experienced any major changes or transitions, such as moving to a new country or experiencing a significant loss?

_____

_____

_____

_____

_____

_____

_____

_____

_____

_____

_____

_____

_____

Are there any family members who are particularly influential or inspirational to you? Why?

_____

_____

_____

_____

_____

_____

_____

_____

_____

What kind of family activities do you enjoy doing together?
Is there a special activity that you no longer do, but wish you did?

_____
_____
_____
_____
_____
_____
_____
_____
_____
_____
_____
_____
_____

How do you stay connected with your family members who live far away?

_____
_____
_____
_____
_____
_____
_____
_____
_____
_____

Information that you want to highlight, ran out of space answering,
or additional information that was not asked or needed more space.

_____

_____

_____

_____

_____

_____

_____

_____

_____

_____

_____

_____

_____

_____

_____

_____

_____

_____

_____

_____

_____

_____

_____

_____

_____

_____

_____

Chapter 4
What Do You Think? And Why?

What do you hope your legacy is?

_____

_____

_____

_____

_____

_____

_____

_____

_____

_____

_____

_____

_____

_____

_____

_____

_____

_____

_____

_____

_____

_____

_____

_____

_____

_____

_____

_____

_____

Is there anything your afraid your legacy is that you don't want it to be?

What are your goals in life?

Did you accomplish them?

What are your biggest regrets in life?
How could you have avoided them?
Or is it better that you learned the lessons you needed to from them?

_____

_____

_____

_____

_____

_____

_____

_____

_____

_____

_____

_____

Who did you impact positively in your life and
how have you made a difference to them?

_____

_____

_____

_____

_____

_____

_____

_____

_____

What are your core values and beliefs? How have they changed over time?

_____

_____

_____

_____

_____

_____

_____

_____

_____

_____

_____

_____

How did your values and beliefs influence your decisions and actions?

_____

_____

_____

_____

_____

_____

_____

_____

_____

What are your greatest accomplishments?

_____

_____

_____

_____

_____

_____

_____

_____

What did you learn from them?

_____

_____

_____

_____

_____

_____

_____

_____

_____

_____

_____

_____

_____

_____

_____

_____

What were your greatest failures?

_____
_____
_____
_____
_____
_____
_____
_____

What have you learned from them?

_____
_____
_____
_____
_____
_____
_____
_____
_____
_____
_____
_____
_____
_____
_____
_____
_____

What have been the most significant turning points in your life?

_____
_____
_____
_____
_____
_____
_____
_____
_____

Why? How have they shaped you as a person?

_____
_____
_____
_____
_____
_____
_____
_____
_____
_____
_____
_____
_____
_____
_____
_____
_____
_____

What is your philosophy on life? How has it evolved over time?

Have you lived a life true to yourself and your beliefs?
Do you feel at times, that you've compromised for others?

Have you made a positive impact on your community and the world around you? How do you continue to do so?

In what ways have you been wronged?

_____
_____
_____
_____
_____
_____
_____
_____

Have you forgiven those who have wronged you?

_____
_____
_____
_____
_____
_____
_____
_____
_____
_____
_____
_____
_____
_____
_____
_____
_____
_____

Have you sought forgiveness from those you have wronged?

_____
_____
_____
_____
_____
_____
_____
_____

Have they forgiven you?

_____
_____
_____
_____
_____
_____
_____
_____
_____
_____
_____
_____
_____
_____
_____
_____
_____

What have been your greatest joys in life?

_____
_____
_____
_____
_____
_____
_____
_____
_____
_____
_____
_____

How can you continue to experience these joys?

_____
_____
_____
_____
_____
_____
_____
_____
_____
_____
_____
_____
_____
_____
_____
_____
_____

How do you take care of your physical health?

_____
_____
_____
_____
_____
_____
_____
_____
_____
_____
_____
_____

How can you continue to do so?

_____
_____
_____
_____
_____
_____
_____
_____
_____
_____

How do you take care of your emotional health?

_____
_____
_____
_____
_____
_____
_____
_____
_____
_____
_____
_____
_____
_____
_____

How can you continue to do so?

_____
_____
_____
_____
_____
_____
_____
_____
_____
_____
_____
_____

How do you take care of your mental health?

_____

_____

_____

_____

_____

_____

_____

_____

_____

_____

_____

_____

_____

How can you continue to do so?

_____

_____

_____

_____

_____

_____

_____

_____

_____

_____

Have you pursued **any** passions and interests? What are they?

_____

_____

_____

_____

_____

_____

_____

_____

_____

_____

_____

Do you continue to do so?

_____

_____

_____

_____

_____

_____

_____

_____

_____

_____

_____

_____

_____

How has pursuing your interests and hobbies benefited you?

Have have you made a positive impact on the environment?

_____

_____

_____

_____

_____

_____

_____

_____

_____

_____

Do you continue to do so?

_____

_____

_____

_____

_____

_____

_____

_____

_____

_____

_____

_____

Have you lived a life of gratitude and appreciation for the blessings in your life? If so, how?

_____

_____

_____

_____

_____

_____

_____

_____

_____

_____

If not, how can you start? Or, how can you continue doing so?

_____

_____

_____

_____

_____

_____

_____

_____

_____

_____

_____

_____

_____

Have you treated others with kindness and compassion? Give some examples:

_____

_____

_____

_____

_____

_____

_____

_____

_____

_____

_____

How can you continue treating others with kindness and compassion?

_____

_____

_____

_____

_____

_____

_____

_____

_____

_____

_____

_____

_____

_____

Have you taken risks and embraced new experiences?
Give some examples how have they shaped you.

_____
_____
_____
_____
_____
_____
_____
_____
_____
_____
_____

What risks do you plan to take in the future?

_____
_____
_____
_____
_____
_____
_____
_____
_____
_____
_____
_____
_____
_____
_____

Have you maintained positive relationships with family and friends?
How can you continue to strengthen those relationships?

_____

_____

_____

_____

_____

_____

_____

_____

_____

_____

_____

_____

Have you lived a life of integrity and honesty?

_____

_____

_____

_____

_____

_____

_____

_____

_____

_____

_____

_____

_____

_____

Have you used your talents and skills to their fullest potential?

_____
_____
_____
_____
_____
_____
_____
_____
_____
_____
_____

Do you continue to develop them? How?

_____
_____
_____
_____
_____
_____
_____
_____
_____
_____
_____
_____
_____
_____
_____
_____

Have you contributed to the betterment of society? If yes, give examples.

_____

_____

_____

_____

_____

_____

_____

_____

_____

_____

_____

How do you continue to contribute to the betterment of society?

_____

_____

_____

_____

_____

_____

_____

_____

_____

_____

_____

_____

_____

Have you lived a life of purpose and meaning?

_____

_____

_____

_____

_____

_____

_____

_____

_____

_____

How do you continue to find fulfillment in your life?

_____

_____

_____

_____

_____

_____

_____

_____

_____

_____

_____

_____

What are your political views? Why?

_____
_____
_____
_____
_____
_____
_____
_____
_____
_____
_____
_____

What is your religious preference?
And how has it affected your life?

_____
_____
_____
_____
_____
_____
_____
_____
_____
_____
_____
_____
_____

Information that you want to highlight, ran out of space answering, or additional information that was not asked or needed more space.

Chapter 5 - Life Lessons

What is the most important lesson you've learned in life so far?

Can you share a time when you made a mistake and learned
a valuable lesson from it?

_____

_____

_____

_____

_____

_____

_____

_____

_____

_____

_____

_____

_____

What values are most important to you?
How have they influenced your life decisions?

_____

_____

_____

_____

_____

_____

_____

_____

_____

_____

Have you ever had a mentor or role model who taught you an important lesson? What was it?

_____

_____

_____

_____

_____

_____

_____

_____

_____

_____

_____

_____

_____

_____

_____

_____

What are some of the biggest risks you've taken in life? What did you learn from them?

_____

_____

_____

_____

_____

_____

_____

_____

_____

_____

_____

What is the most important lesson you've learned in life so far?

What values are most important to you?
How have they influenced your life decisions?

_____

_____

_____

_____

_____

_____

_____

_____

_____

_____

_____

_____

_____

_____

_____

_____

_____

_____

_____

_____

_____

_____

_____

_____

Can you share a time when you faced a failure or setback?
How did you grow from it?

How do you handle difficult situations or decisions in your life, and what have you learned from those experiences?

_____
_____
_____
_____
_____
_____
_____
_____
_____
_____
_____
_____
_____
_____
_____
_____
_____
_____
_____
_____
_____
_____
_____
_____
_____
_____

What is something you once believed to be true, but later discovered was false?
How did you learn that lesson?

_____

_____

_____

_____

_____

_____

_____

_____

_____

_____

_____

Can you share a time when you had to confront your fears?
What did you learn from the experience?

_____

_____

_____

_____

_____

_____

_____

_____

_____

_____

_____

_____

What is the most valuable piece of advice you've ever received?
How has it impacted your life?

How have your life experiences shaped your perspectives on the
world and the people around you?

_____

_____

_____

_____

_____

_____

_____

_____

_____

_____

_____

What is the most important lesson you've learned about relationships?
(Romantic, familial, or platonic)

_____

_____

_____

_____

_____

_____

_____

_____

_____

_____

_____

_____

_____

Can you share a time when you had to make a difficult
decision that taught you an important lesson?

_____

_____

_____

_____

_____

_____

_____

_____

_____

_____

How have your past failures or mistakes helped you become a better person?

_____

_____

_____

_____

_____

_____

_____

_____

_____

_____

_____

_____

What is your philosophy on life? How did you develop it?

_____
_____
_____
_____
_____
_____
_____
_____
_____
_____
_____
_____
_____
_____
_____
_____
_____
_____
_____
_____
_____
_____
_____
_____
_____
_____
_____
_____

What are some of the biggest challenges you've faced?
How have you overcome them?

_____

_____

_____

_____

_____

_____

_____

_____

_____

_____

_____

_____

_____

_____

_____

_____

_____

_____

_____

_____

_____

_____

_____

_____

_____

_____

_____

_____

Can you share a time when you had to face criticism or rejection?
What did you learn from it?

What is the most important lesson you've learned about
self-care and personal well-being?

_____
_____
_____
_____
_____
_____
_____
_____
_____
_____
_____
_____
_____
_____
_____
_____
_____
_____
_____
_____
_____
_____
_____
_____
_____
_____
_____

How have you learned to cope with stress and adversity in your life?

What is the most significant change you've experienced in your life?
How did it shape you?

_____

_____

_____

_____

_____

_____

_____

_____

_____

_____

_____

_____

_____

_____

_____

_____

_____

_____

_____

_____

_____

_____

_____

_____

What is the most important lesson you've learned about success and achievement?

How have your experiences and lessons learned shaped your goals and aspirations for the future?

_____

_____

_____

_____

_____

_____

_____

_____

_____

Can you share a time when you had to step outside your comfort zone? Did it teach you an important lesson?

_____

_____

_____

_____

_____

_____

_____

_____

_____

_____

_____

_____

GENERAL

What keeps you up at night?

_____

_____

_____

_____

_____

_____

_____

What makes you feel successful?

_____

_____

_____

_____

_____

_____

_____

_____

_____

_____

_____

_____

_____

_____

What is one thing for which you want to be remembered?

_____

_____

_____

_____

_____

_____

_____

_____

_____

Is money important to you, why or why not?

_____

_____

_____

_____

_____

_____

_____

_____

_____

_____

_____

_____

_____

_____

_____

_____

What are you most passionate about?

How do you define risk?

If money were not an issue, what would you be doing with your time?

_____

_____

_____

_____

_____

_____

_____

_____

If you could only accomplish one thing in this process, what would it be?

_____

_____

_____

_____

_____

_____

_____

_____

_____

_____

_____

_____

_____

FAMILY

For whom are you financially responsible?

_____

_____

_____

_____

_____

_____

_____

_____

_____

If something happens to you, what preparations have you made for those people?

_____

_____

_____

_____

_____

_____

_____

_____

_____

_____

_____

_____

_____

_____

_____

_____

For whom might you have other potential responsibilities?
For example, will you be a caregiver to a parent?

_____

_____

_____

_____

_____

_____

_____

_____

_____

Do you want to be involved in the financial lives of your
children or grandchildren?

_____

_____

_____

_____

_____

_____

_____

_____

_____

_____

_____

_____

_____

_____

_____

What type of legacy do you want to leave your children and grandchildren?

_____
_____
_____
_____
_____
_____
_____
_____
_____

How do you want them to remember you?

_____
_____
_____
_____
_____
_____
_____
_____
_____
_____
_____
_____
_____
_____
_____

What values do you want to pass on?

_____

_____

_____

_____

_____

_____

_____

_____

What do your spouse and children find important?
How can you help them achieve their goals?

_____

_____

_____

_____

_____

_____

_____

_____

_____

_____

_____

_____

_____

_____

CHARITY

What are you passionate about?

_____
_____
_____
_____
_____
_____
_____
_____
_____
_____
_____
_____
_____
_____
_____
_____
_____
_____
_____
_____
_____
_____
_____
_____
_____
_____
_____

Do you want to share that passion with your family?

_____

_____

_____

_____

_____

_____

_____

_____

_____

Do you want to be recognized for your giving or to remain anonymous?

_____

_____

_____

_____

_____

_____

_____

_____

_____

_____

Do you want to create a legacy and expectations of giving for your family?

_____

_____

_____

_____

_____

_____

_____

_____

How important to you are the tax advantages you could get
from some forms of charitable giving?

_____

_____

_____

_____

_____

_____

_____

_____

_____

_____

_____

_____

_____

_____

HUMAN CAPITAL

How are you investing in yourself and your family?

_____

_____

_____

_____

_____

_____

_____

_____

_____

_____

Education _____

_____

_____

_____

_____

_____

_____

Health _____

_____

_____

_____

_____

_____

_____

Do you want to incorporate travel in your human capital plan?
Would that travel include other generations of your family?

_____

_____

_____

_____

_____

_____

_____

_____

Do you want to create a legacy of investing in the human
capital of future generations of your family?

_____

_____

_____

_____

_____

_____

_____

_____

_____

_____

_____

_____

_____

FINANCE

Have you selected a financial team and coach?

_____

_____

_____

_____

_____

Do they have the credentials and experience you are looking for?
If so, what credentials were important to you?
Do you know what those credentials mean?
Do you understand the different types of advisors?

_____

_____

_____

_____

_____

_____

_____

_____

_____

_____

_____

_____

_____

_____

How have you been continuing your own financial education?
(Note: This does not have to be formal, and your team could provide it.)

_____

_____

_____

_____

_____

_____

_____

_____

_____

_____

Are you preparing your family for the financial legacy that you plan to leave to them?
(Note: this is important whether you are leaving great wealth or relatively little.)

_____

_____

_____

_____

_____

_____

_____

_____

_____

_____

_____

_____

_____

_____

_____

_____

To maintain your ideal lifestyle, how much income do you need?

_____

_____

_____

_____

_____

_____

_____

_____

_____

_____

_____

_____

_____

_____

_____

_____

_____

_____

_____

_____

_____

_____

_____

_____

_____

What is your current financial situation, including your assets and liabilities?

If you own a business, do you have a plan for its succession?

_____

_____

_____

_____

_____

_____

_____

_____

_____

_____

Who do you want to inherit your assets after you pass away?

_____

_____

_____

_____

_____

_____

_____

_____

_____

_____

_____

_____

_____

_____

Do you have a will? If not, do you need one?

_____

_____

_____

_____

_____

_____

_____

_____

Who do you want to be the executor of your will?

_____

_____

_____

_____

_____

_____

_____

_____

_____

_____

_____

_____

_____

Do you want to donate any of your assets to charity?

_____

_____

_____

_____

_____

_____

_____

_____

Do you have any minor children or dependents who need
to be taken care of after you pass away?

_____

_____

_____

_____

_____

_____

_____

_____

_____

_____

_____

_____

Who do you want to be the guardian of your minor children?

_____

_____

_____

_____

_____

_____

_____

_____

Do you have (or want to set up) a trust for any of your assets?

_____

_____

_____

_____

_____

_____

_____

_____

_____

_____

_____

_____

_____

_____

Who do you want to be the trustee of your trust?

_____

_____

Do you have any special needs children who will need to be taken care of after
you pass away? If so, who do you want to be the caretaker of
your special needs children?

_____

_____

_____

_____

_____

_____

_____

_____

Do you have any life insurance policies, and who are the beneficiaries?

_____

_____

_____

_____

_____

_____

_____

_____

_____

_____

_____

Do you have any retirement accounts or pension plans?
Who are the beneficiaries?

_____

_____

_____

_____

_____

_____

_____

_____

_____

Do you have any real estate?
Who do you want to inherit it?

_____

_____

_____

_____

_____

_____

_____

_____

_____

_____

_____

_____

_____

_____

_____

Do you own any businesses?
Who do you want to take over ownership after you pass away?

_____

_____

_____

_____

_____

_____

_____

_____

Do you want to leave any instructions for your funeral or burial?

_____

_____

_____

_____

_____

_____

_____

_____

_____

_____

_____

_____

_____

Do you have any debts that need to be paid off after you pass away?

_____

_____

_____

_____

_____

_____

_____

_____

Do you want to leave any specific gifts or bequests to
individuals or organizations?

_____

_____

_____

_____

_____

_____

_____

_____

_____

_____

Do you have any digital assets, such as social media accounts or
online banking accounts?

Do you have any pets?
Who do you want to take care of them after you pass away?

_____

_____

_____

_____

_____

_____

_____

_____

_____

Do you want to establish a power of attorney to make financial or medical
decisions for you if you become incapacitated?

_____

_____

_____

_____

_____

_____

_____

_____

_____

_____

_____

_____

_____

_____

_____

Do you want to establish a living will or advance directive to specify your medical wishes if you become incapacitated?

_____

_____

_____

_____

_____

_____

_____

_____

_____

Do you want to establish a healthcare proxy to make medical decisions for you if you become incapacitated?

_____

_____

_____

_____

_____

_____

_____

_____

_____

_____

_____

_____

_____

_____

Have you discussed your estate planning wishes with your loved ones and appointed them as your agents in necessary documents?

Information that you want to highlight, ran out of space answering, or additional information that was not asked or needed more space.

Chapter 6 - Pulling it together, What does it all mean? The final set of questions.

The Big Questions

What are the take aways you got from completing this book?

What is the take away you hope the person who reads your answers gets?

What lessons do you want to reinforce? Why?

What is your biggest wish for the reader of your answers?

Tell a story that that you think is important that this book didn't cover:

What 5 questions do you wish the book asked?
What would your answers have been?

Information that you want to highlight, ran out of space answering, or
additional information that was not asked or needed more space.

_____

_____

_____

_____

_____

_____

_____

_____

_____

_____

_____

_____

_____

_____

_____

_____

_____

_____

_____

_____

_____

_____

_____

_____

_____

_____

_____

_____

Chapter 7 - Appendix

Where is the following information found?

Deeds

_____

Birth Certificate

_____

Marriage License

_____

Safe Deposit Box location

_____

Social Media Accounts and Passwords

_____

_____

Power of Attorneys

_____

Life Insurance

_____

I have accounts at:

Banks

_____

Investments

_____

IRAs

_____

401k(s)

_____

Annuities

_____

Insurance

_____

Credit cards

_____

Other loans

_____

I have the following real estate:

Home

_____

Rentals

_____

Other

_____

I have private assets that are included on a statement such as

_____

_____

_____

_____

The professionals I works with are::

Financial

_____

Person/team

_____

Firm

_____

Banker

_____

CPA

_____

Insurance agent

_____

Employer

_____

Other

_____

People who know about this book

_____

Last Wishes:

_____

_____

_____

_____

_____

_____

_____

_____

_____

_____

_____

_____

_____

_____

_____

_____

_____

_____

_____

_____

_____

_____

_____

_____

_____

_____

_____

_____

_____

_____

_____

_____

_____

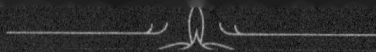

Any last thoughts?

Extra pages to be used as needed:
(Ideas include family recipes, various stories, thoughts you want included –
basically anything you want)